ELLA JOHNSON MEMORIAL PUB. DISTRICT

3 8514   2179

W9-BEM-371

SEP   2009

CH REF
Cj 423.9 WIM

**Childrens Reference
Does Not Circulate**

**ELLA JOHNSON MEMORIAL
PUBLIC LIBRARY DISTRICT**

109 S. STATE ST.

HAMPSHIRE, IL 60140

(847) 683-4490

DEMCO

THIS LAND CALLED AMERICA: **FLORIDA**

CREATIVE EDUCATION

Published by Creative Education
P.O. Box 227, Mankato, Minnesota 56002
Creative Education is an imprint of The Creative Company
www.thecreativecompany.us

Book and cover design by Blue Design (www.bluedes.com)
Art direction by Rita Marshall
Printed in the United States of America

Photographs by Alamy (Dennis Hallinan), Corbis (Atlantide Pho-
totravel, Carlos Barria/Reuters, Bettmann, Blaine Harrington III, Janet
Jarman, Stuart Westmorland), Getty Images (Altrendo Nature, Eddie
Brady, Mike Brinson, Pascal Crapet, Loomis Dean//Time Life Pictures,
Jeff Foott, Stephen Frink, Mitchell Funk, Bill Heinsohn, George Hunter,
Kean Collection, MPI, Chris Newbert, Panoramic Images, Photogra-
pher's Choice, Raedle, BRUCE WEAVER/AFP)

Copyright © 2009 Creative Education
International copyright reserved in all countries. No part of this book
may be reproduced in any form without written permission from the
publisher.

Library of Congress Cataloging-in-Publication Data
Wimmer, Teresa.
Florida / by Teresa Wimmer.
p. cm. — (This land called America)
Includes bibliographical references and index.
ISBN 978-1-58341-634-1
1. Florida—Juvenile literature. I. Title. II. Series.
F311.3.W56 2008
975.9—dc22   2007015004

First Edition
9 8 7 6 5 4 3 2 1

This Land Called America

FLORIDA

Teresa Wimmer

Florida

TERESA WIMMER

ON A HOT DAY IN MIAMI, PEOPLE CANNOT
WAIT TO HEAD TO THE BEACH. THE SAND IS SO
BRIGHT, IT SHINES LIKE GOLD. A FEW PEOPLE GRAB
THEIR SURFBOARDS AND PADDLE OUT INTO THE
ATLANTIC OCEAN. WHEN A BIG WAVE COMES,
THEY RIDE IT INLAND. FARTHER OUT, SCUBA
DIVERS PLUNGE TO THE BOTTOM OF THE OCEAN.
AWAY FROM THE WATER, TOURISTS SPREAD THEIR
BLANKETS ON THE SAND AND BASK IN THE SUN'S
WARMTH. CHILDREN RUN ALONG THE SHORE
AND COLLECT SEASHELLS. THEY WATCH THE PALM
TREES SWAY IN THE BREEZE AND LOOK OUT AT ALL
THE BEAUTY FLORIDA HAS TO OFFER.

YEAR

1513 Spanish explorer Juan Ponce de León lands in Florida and claims it for Spain.

EVENT

Seminole and Español

THOUSANDS OF YEARS AGO, THE PANZACOLA, APALACHI-
COLA, AND APALACHEE AMERICAN INDIAN TRIBES ARRIVED
IN THE LAND NOW KNOWN AS FLORIDA. THEY SPOKE DIF-
FERENT LANGUAGES AND SOMETIMES FOUGHT WITH ONE
ANOTHER. THEY LIVED IN SMALL HUTS MADE OF BRANCHES
AND COVERED WITH HARD MUD AND CLAY. DURING THE
WINTER, THEY HUNTED DEER, SQUIRRELS, RACCOONS,

Juan Ponce de León

and rabbits. In the summer, they fished, gathered shellfish from the Atlantic Ocean, and grew crops such as beans and corn.

In 1513, Spanish explorer Juan Ponce de León landed on the northeastern coast of Florida. He came looking for the fountain of youth because he hoped that drinking its magical water would make him young again. Impressed by the many vibrant flowers he saw in the new land, he named it *La Florida*, which means "the flowery land" in Spanish.

More Spaniards followed Ponce de León, hoping to find gold, gems, and precious minerals. But they were unsuccessful. Many of the Spanish explorers, called conquistadors, had a

Three hundred years after Juan Ponce de León discovered Florida, American colonists would come into conflict with native peoples (opposite).

YEAR
1581   The first African American slaves are brought to St. Augustine.
EVENT

State bird: mockingbird

hard time living with the Indians. The explorers treated the Indians badly and repeatedly tried to take their land. Florida was also very hot and full of mosquitoes and strange creatures such as alligators. Many Spaniards did not live long in such an environment.

One of the Spanish explorers, however, did manage to survive in Florida for a while. In 1565, Pedro Menéndez de Avilés founded the city of St. Augustine. It was the first permanent European settlement and is the oldest city in the United States.

Avilés wanted to turn the Indians into Catholics. He brought Spanish priests with him, and they built churches called missions in northern Florida. Sometimes the Indians were killed if they refused to adopt Catholicism. Eventually, many Indians did become Catholics. They also learned how to raise cattle, weave, and read and write in Spanish. But they still kept many of their Indian customs.

Many Spaniards had a hard time earning a living in Florida. The soil along the coast was not good for growing crops, so they were forced to move farther inland. This left the coastal areas open to invasions from other countries.

Spanish priests and missionaries visited Indian villages regularly to preach about religion.

YEAR

1763   Florida is divided into East and West Florida after the French and Indian War.

EVENT

Seminole leader Osceola fought against U.S. soldiers until he was captured in St. Augustine in 1837.

Florida orange harvest

In the late 1700s, the British came to Florida. The Spanish got Indian tribes from other states to help them fight off the British. These Indian tribes joined together and became the Seminoles. "Seminole" means "runaway," or "outlaw."

In the 1800s, white people from northern states and Europe came to Florida. They needed land to live on and to farm. In the 1820s, General Andrew Jackson tried to force the Seminoles to give up their land. A leader named Osceola advised the Seminoles as they fought against the U.S. for many years. Eventually, most of the Indians were pushed far south or out west.

Florida became a state in 1845. Afterward, thousands of people from northern states moved to Florida to buy land and sell it. They soon found out that a lot of the land was swampy and hit by hurricanes. But it was also good land for growing fruit. In the 1900s, citrus fruit such as oranges became an important product of Florida. The oranges were shipped all across the country on trains.

YEAR
1783 Florida's first newspaper, the *East-Florida Gazette*, begins publication.
EVENT

Forests, Swamps, and Storms

MILLIONS OF YEARS AGO, FLORIDA WAS UNDERNEATH THE ATLANTIC OCEAN. THEN, SOME OF THE WATER RECEDED, AND FLORIDA EMERGED. TO THE WEST, FLORIDA SHARES A BORDER WITH ALABAMA. ON ITS NORTHERN SIDE ARE ALABAMA AND GEORGIA. THE REST OF FLORIDA IS SURROUNDED BY WATER, WITH THE ATLANTIC OCEAN TO THE EAST AND THE GULF OF MEXICO TO THE WEST.

Northern Florida is known as the panhandle because it is shaped like a pan's handle. The area is covered by forests. Beech, holly, magnolia, and oak trees draped with Spanish moss grow in the fertile soil. The area along the western panhandle is called the Emerald Coast because of its bright green water bordered by sandy beaches. A mineral called quartz in the sand makes it crunch when people walk on it.

Near the capital city of Tallahassee flow the Wakulla Springs. They are some of the world's largest, deepest, and clearest freshwater springs. The warm springs pump thousands of gallons of warm water into the Wakulla River. Alligators like the warm water. They have even attacked people who tried to swim in their river!

Central Florida produces most of the state's orange crop. Oranges need sunshine and warmth to grow. The weather here is usually warm, even in winter. In the spring, the trees blossom and fill the air with the tangy, sweet smell of oranges. But sometimes cold spells come and freeze the oranges before they can be picked.

In Wakulla Springs State Park, people can take guided boat tours on the Wakulla River.

Long and beardlike, Spanish moss that grows on trees thrives in Florida's humid climate.

YEAR
1816
Andrew Jackson invades Florida and battles the Seminoles, starting the First Seminole War.
EVENT

S outh-central Florida is known as the Heartland. Farms growing corn, carrots, beans, and tomatoes are spread over the rolling hills and flat lands. Strawberries and green rows of sugar cane are plentiful here, too. All of these products paint the landscape in bright colors.

Lake Okeechobee, Florida's largest lake, is found in the Heartland. At 730 square miles (1,890 sq km), it is larger than any U.S. lake except the Great Lakes of the North and Utah's Great Salt Lake. Fish such as bass, bluegills, and catfish swim here. Bald eagles, storks, and manatees also call the lake home.

Like Lake Okeechobee in Florida's Heartland, a region known for its strawberries (above), Florida Bay (opposite) is home to such aquatic creatures as manatees and sea turtles.

1851   Florida's first colleges, Florida State University and the University of Florida, are founded.

The largest island of the Florida Keys is Key Largo, in whose coral-filled waters swim many colorful fish.

The southern part of Florida is covered by the most famous area of Florida wetlands, the Everglades. Marshes, swamps, lakes, and rivers make up the area. Small islands of mangrove trees dot the waters. Many living things thrive there, including herons, spoonbills, turtles, fish, panthers, and, of course, alligators.

At the southern tip of Florida lies a chain of small islands known as the Florida Keys. Key West is the country's southern-most city. Off the coast of the Keys grow unusual coral reefs. A coral reef is a limestone cluster made up of the skeletons of millions of tiny sea creatures. The brightly colored reefs look like fans and branches. Tropical fish swim around the reefs, too. They create a lively underwater world.

Some of the wildest weather in the country strikes Florida. Storms such as hurricanes pound Florida more often than any other state. In 1992, Hurricane Andrew hit southern Florida. It destroyed many homes and buildings. A few people were even killed. Florida winters are usually dry. Northern Florida can get snow, but not very much. In summer, the weather all over the state is hot and humid.

The Seven Mile Bridge is one of about 50 bridges that connect the islands of the Florida Keys.

Workers begin draining marshes in the Everglades to create more farmland.

A Mixed Bag

OVER THE PAST FEW DECADES, MORE AND MORE PEOPLE FROM ALL OVER THE WORLD HAVE MADE THEIR HOME IN FLORIDA. THEY COME FOR THE SUNNY SKIES, THE WARM WATERS, AND THE MANY DIFFERENT JOBS THAT FLORIDA PROVIDES.

Hundreds of years ago, Spanish explorers brought the first Africans to Florida as Slaves. When they were freed, they sometimes married white people or Indians. Later, many worked in the fields picking fruit or chopping down sugar cane.

In the 1800s, people from European countries such as Portugal, Italy, and Romania immigrated to Florida. They came to work in the fields, lumber mills, and factories. Some Cuban immigrants built cigar-making factories.

Today, white people make up the majority in Florida. Hispanic people and African Americans are next. Many people from Mexico and Central American countries such as Guatemala and Nicaragua continue to flock to Florida.

Immigrants to Florida and the rest of the U.S. can become citizens through a process called naturalization.

The city of West Palm Beach was developed in the early 1900s and quickly became a popular resort center.

The John F. Kennedy Space Center has launched all of America's human space flight missions.

Many Americans retire in Naples, a popular city in southwestern Florida along the Gulf of Mexico.

All of the Cubans and other Hispanic people have made the Spanish influence in Florida very strong. Many corporations have built their Latin American headquarters in Miami. In Tampa Bay and Miami, signs are written in both English and Spanish. The *Miami Herald* newspaper even publishes a separate Spanish edition.

Many people still work in Florida's factories, farms, and orange groves. They work in food processing plants and printing companies. At Cape Canaveral's Kennedy Space Center, many work in the aerospace industry. They build and launch shuttles into space. Some of Florida's biggest employers are hospitals, schools, banks, and insurance companies.

YEAR

1906 A hurricane batters the Florida Keys and Miami, killing hundreds of people.

EVENT

1929   The Mediterranean fruit fly invades Florida's citrus groves, severely damaging the orange crop.

Sharp-toothed and thick-skinned, moray eels like living in the warm, shallow waters of the Florida Keys.

Moray eel

Visitors today have the railroads built by Henry Morrison Flagler to thank for helping bring them there. In 1883, Flagler arrived in St. Augustine but found the city hard to access. So he built a railroad that ran through cities up and down the eastern coast. The trains carried visitors into Florida and farm products and fish out to other states. Flagler built big, beautiful hotels, too.

Because so many visitors arrive in Florida each year, the tourism industry employs many people. During spring break, college students come to the beaches of Panama City and Daytona Beach. Theme parks such as Walt Disney World, Universal Studios, and Busch Gardens-Africa employ thousands of people. Other people work in the many stores, hotels, and resorts nearby.

Florida also has a long artistic past. In 1928, author Ernest Hemingway moved to Key West. He loved the warmth, flowers, and access to fishing, and decided to live there for a few years. In Key West, he wrote some of his most famous short stories. In 1952, while living in Cuba, he published *The Old Man and the Sea,* a short novel about an old Cuban fisherman. The book won Hemingway many awards.

American author Ernest Hemingway enjoyed life in Key West during the late 1920s and 1930s.

YEAR
1937   Pilot Amelia Earhart flies out of Miami on her way to complete a flight around the world.
EVENT

- 23 -

D uring the winter months, many retired people go to Florida to escape the snow and cold of the northern states. Some stay just for the winter, but others make their homes there. The many golf courses, restaurants, beaches, and cruises provide endless entertainment. Some of the richest families in America live in Palm Beach, Boca Raton, and Naples.

Because so many people live in the state, overcrowding and poverty have become problems. Florida also has one of the highest crime rates in the nation. But people are working hard to make it a safe and successful place for everyone.

Whether people go to the beach to surf (above) or take in seaside views while playing golf (opposite), Florida's lengthy coastline offers plenty of enjoyment.

YEAR

1961   Astronaut Alan Shepard, aboard a rocket from Cape Canaveral, becomes the first American in space.

EVENT

Sun, Fun, and Mickey

FLORIDIANS TAKE PRIDE IN EVERYTHING THEIR STATE HAS TO OFFER. THE ENDLESS BEACHES AND WATER PROVIDE PLENTY OF CHANCES TO SURF, SWIM, FISH, AND BOAT. BECAUSE OF THE WARM WEATHER, GOLFERS AND TENNIS PLAYERS CAN PLAY THROUGHOUT THE YEAR. MANY WORLD-FAMOUS ATHLETES, SUCH AS PROFESSIONAL GOLFER TIGER WOODS, CALL FLORIDA HOME.

Even the land Florida sits on is unique. Most of the U.S. sits on solid marble, granite, and slate foundations. But Florida sits on top of limestone, a softer, more fragile rock. That is because Florida was underwater more recently than the rest of the country. Sand, silt, and shells from the ocean formed the limestone layers.

The beaches between St. Augustine and Daytona Beach are among the few in the country that people are allowed to drive on. They are wide and made of hard-packed sand. Because of the potential danger to people and nature, some people want to restrict driving on these beaches.

A local tradition since the early 1900s, driving on Daytona Beach is still done in certain sections.

Cinderella's Castle is perhaps the most recognizable feature of Orlando's Walt Disney World complex.

The slow-moving manatee frequents Florida's waters and can stay underwater for up to 20 minutes.

Pirates once roamed Florida's southern beaches and waters. Today, scuba divers and treasure hunters troll the waters where pirate ships once sank. They go looking for gold and other buried treasures. Each January, Tampa holds the Gasparilla Pirate Fest. Men dressed as pirates sail into Tampa and parade through its downtown.

Near Key Largo, scuba divers can spend a night underwater at Jules' Undersea Lodge. The hotel sits 21 feet (6 m) below the sea and was once used as a research laboratory. Large windows line the hotel's two public spaces. Visitors can watch the undersea world all night, if they want to.

When many people think of Florida, they think of Walt Disney World. The huge resort includes four different theme parks: Epcot, Hollywood Studios, Animal Kingdom Park, and Magic Kingdom Park. Each year, millions of people experience the adventure of such attractions as Mission: SPACE, the Tower of Terror, Expedition Everest, and Splash Mountain.

At Orlando's Universal Studios, visitors can participate in rides taken straight from the movies. They can zap aliens in Men in Black: Alien Attack. On Jaws, a huge mechanical shark threatens to eat people. The rides make people feel as though they are part of the movies.

Miami Beach, Florida

YEAR

1980   The Mariel Boatlift—a mass exodus of 125,000 Cubans from Mariel, Cuba, to Florida—occurs.

EVENT

Since 1945, Miami Beach has turned into a luxury-resort area and popular tourist destination.

YEAR

2000 After several recounts of Florida ballots, George W. Bush wins the U.S. presidency by a narrow margin.

EVENT

QUICK FACTS

Population: 18,089,888

Largest city: Jacksonville (pop. 773,781)

Capital: Tallahassee

Entered the union: March 3, 1845

Nickname: Sunshine State

State flower: orange blossom

State bird: mockingbird

Size: 65,755 sq mi (170,305 sq km)—22nd-biggest in U.S.

Major industries: manufacturing, farming, tourism

Sea World Orlando allows visitors to get a close-up look at dolphins, manatees, sharks, and other sea creatures. Shamu the killer whale dances, leaps, and dives for cheering crowds. Sea World's Beached Animal Rescue and Rehabilitation Program has saved many endangered animals, including manatees, dolphins, and sea turtles.

Florida's animals, historical figures, and attractions lend their names to many of the state's professional sports teams. Fans can cheer for the National Football League's Jacksonville Jaguars, Tampa Bay Buccaneers, and Miami Dolphins. The Orlando Magic and Miami Heat play basketball, while the Florida Marlins and Tampa Bay Rays play Major League Baseball. The year 2003 was monumental for Florida teams. The Buccaneers won the Super Bowl, and the Marlins won the World Series.

It is no wonder that Floridians take pride in their state. Few states in the country can boast as many different attractions, sports, people, and animals as Florida. From the Emerald Coast to the Gold Coast, people will always enjoy basking in the warmth of the "Sunshine State."

YEAR

2007   Republican Charley Crist becomes the 44th governor of Florida.

EVENT

BIBLIOGRAPHY

Chang, Perry. *Florida*. New York: Benchmark Books, 1998.

College of Education, University of South Florida. "Famous Floridians: Ernest Hemingway." Exploring Florida: A Social Studies Resource for Students and Teachers. http://fcit.usf.edu/florida/lessons/hemingway/hemingway.htm.

Florida Tourism Industry Marketing Corporation. "Homepage." Visit Florida. http://www.visitflorida.com/.

Gannon, Michael. *Florida: A Short History*. Gainesville, Fla.: University Press of Florida, 1993.

State of Florida. "Florida History." MyFlorida.com. http://dhr.dos.state.fl.us/kids/history.cfm.

Walton, Chelle Koster. *Florida*. Oakland, Calif.: Fodor's Travel Publications, 1998.

INDEX